HOW CAN I BENEFIT FROM
MY BAPTISM?

✕ CULTIVATING BIBLICAL GODLINESS

Series Editors

Joel R. Beeke and Ryan M. McGraw

Dr. D. Martyn Lloyd-Jones once said that what the church needs to do most of all is "to begin herself to live the Christian life. If she did that, men and women would be crowding into our buildings. They would say, 'What is the secret of this?'" As Christians, one of our greatest needs is for the Spirit of God to cultivate biblical godliness in us in order to put the beauty of Christ on display through us, all to the glory of the triune God. With this goal in mind, this series of booklets treats matters vital to Christian experience at a basic level. Each booklet addresses a specific question in order to inform the mind, warm the affections, and transform the whole person by the Spirit's grace, so that the church may adorn the doctrine of God our Savior in all things.

HOW CAN I BENEFIT FROM
MY BAPTISM?

IAN MACLEOD

REFORMATION HERITAGE BOOKS
GRAND RAPIDS, MICHIGAN

How Can I Benefit from My Baptism?
© 2019 by Ian Macleod

Reformation Heritage Books
2965 Leonard St. NE
Grand Rapids, MI 49525
616-977-0889
orders@heritagebooks.org
www.heritagebooks.org

Printed in the United States of America
19 20 21 22 23 24/10 9 8 7 6 5 4 3 2 1

ISBN 978-1-60178-644-9
ISBN 978-1-60178-645-6 (e-pub)

For additional Reformed literature, request a free book list from Reformation Heritage Books at the above regular or e-mail address.

HOW CAN I BENEFIT FROM
MY BAPTISM?

But the mercy of the LORD is from everlasting to everlasting upon them that fear him, and his righteousness unto children's children; to such as keep his covenant, and to those that remember his commandments to do them.

—Psalm 103:17–18

That there is great value and benefit in Christian baptism should be an obvious truth to anyone who takes the Word of God seriously. We see baptism's value when we consider the person who instituted it—the Lord Jesus (Matt. 28:19). We recognize its obvious value in that the Most High God is showing Himself willing to covenant with sinful man in grace (Gen. 17:7–10; cf. Acts 2:39). Its benefits become apparent when we consider the great gospel blessings signified and sealed in baptism—union with Christ (Gal. 3:27), the washing away of sins by His blood (Mark 1:4), regeneration by the Spirit (Titus 3:5), the Father's adopting love (Gal. 3:26), and newness of life (Rom. 6:3–4).

For all that is obvious, however, what does not seem as obvious is the answer to the question, How can I benefit from my baptism? In question 167, the Westminster Larger Catechism refers to this as "the needful but much neglected duty of improving our baptism." These questions ought to impress our consciences: How have I profited from baptism? Can I profit from it more? In many cases, the benefits of baptism have been stunted or canceled through abuse. On the one hand, to claim or suggest that the waters of baptism automatically effect the forgiveness of sins is a dangerous delusion. To presume that regeneration inevitably accompanies or follows baptism is equally dangerous. On the other hand, regarding baptism merely as a profession of personal faith robs the sacrament of its deep spiritual meaning and benefit. If the Larger Catechism is correct, then arguably the greatest culprit for not benefiting from baptism is either neglect or lacking awareness of what the Scriptures teach about baptism. The best ways to remedy these problems are, first, to understand the benefits of baptism and, second, to know how we benefit from baptism.

AN ILLUSTRATION: FROM RAGS TO RICHES

In many ways, the baptized person is like a beggar who has come into a tremendous inheritance of a great and stately mansion and incredible wealth. Before, because of his own sloth, neglect, immorality, and crime, he was bankrupt; he trudged around the streets in his old clothes, he had no work, he begged for money, and he had no friends or family who cared for him. He was a loner, a reject in and out of prison and despised by one and all. "Such were some of you," Paul says to the Corinthians. "You stole, you lied, you cheated, you abused and were abused, you slept around, you did everything that excluded you from the kingdom of God." "But," he continues, "you were washed, you were sanctified, you were justified in the name of the Lord Jesus and by the Spirit of our God" (see 1 Cor. 6:9–11). And so this washed beggar is brought from the vile squalor in the streets of sin and from spiritual bankruptcy into "an inheritance incorruptible, and undefiled, and that fadeth not away" (1 Peter 1:4). Incredible benefits are now his! As he goes on in life, he learns more and more of the good things he has inherited, and as he grows in this knowledge he benefits more and more from these things with each passing day.

This is a small picture of how baptism serves as a means of grace in the believer's life. The gospel benefits signified and sealed in baptism have brought the lost and spiritually bankrupt sinner into a great inheritance, a great treasure house of blessing. Incredible benefits are now his! As he goes on in life, he learns more and more of the good things that he has inherited in Christ, and he profits (or should profit) more and more from these things with each passing day. Hence, the Larger Catechism continues, "The needful but much neglected duty of improving our baptism, *is to be performed by us all our life long*" (emphasis added). Wilhelmus à Brakel exhorts, "Be reminded of your baptism as often as you hear your name mentioned."[1] Baptism happens only once, but the benefits derived from baptism through faith in Christ and with the Spirit's blessing are lifelong.

So what are the benefits of baptism, and how do I benefit from it? In answering these questions, we will follow the life of the beggar who has come into this great inheritance, together with his children. He benefits from his baptism in each of the following ways.

BY RECOGNIZING WHAT GOD HAS DONE FOR ME IN CHRIST

Louis Berkhof wrote helpfully, "We are no richer than our comprehension of what we possess, and that it is the true appreciation of our wealth which determines the measure of enjoyment derived from it."[2] The beggar might be walking around the grand halls of his new mansion completely unaware of or unappreciative of all the luxuries and wealth

---

1. Wilhelmus à Brakel, *The Christian's Reasonable Service* (Grand Rapids: Reformation Heritage Books, 1999), 2:521. Brakel is referring to the custom of his day that the child's name was first pronounced at the time of his or her baptism, and when the child's name was pronounced, the name of the Lord was also pronounced; thereby the Lord appropriated the child to Himself.

2. Louis Berkhof and Cornelius Van Til, *Foundations of Christian Education: Addresses to Christian Teachers* (Phillipsburg, N.J.: P&R, 1990), 79.

available to him. Indeed, he may walk around the lush gardens and be as miserable as he ever was on the street. If he does not comprehend or appreciate his wealth, then he does not receive enjoyment from it, and it is as though he were still living in poverty. What a tragic thing it is when Christians don't comprehend or appreciate the riches of grace that have been signified and sealed to them in baptism. It can be as though they were not inheritors of a tremendous spiritual inheritance.

Baptism, however, helps me recognize what I was before grace and what has been done for me in Christ (1 Cor. 6:7–10; Eph. 2:1–7). In this regard, baptism is both a sign and a seal. A sign points to something else; it is not the thing itself. A sign on the road might tell you that you are twenty miles from Jerusalem; the sign is not Jerusalem, but the sign points you to Jerusalem. So baptism signifies Christ and all the blessings and promises of the covenant of grace in Him. The seal, however, is the mark of authentication. How do you know the sign is true? How do you know it will be true for you? How do you know this is not all too good to be true? Because along with the sign, there is also the authenticating seal of the king. Baptism points us to the tremendous blessings and promises of the covenant of grace, but it is also the authenticating seal of God. Therefore, all the blessings signified are real and available to me according to the terms of the covenant of grace.

What then is signified and sealed in baptism? The washing of water points to the filth and pollution of our sin and that we need to be washed. Baptism into the triune name signifies and seals our identification with each of the divine persons. Being baptized into the name of the Father signifies and seals the great and eternal covenant of grace that God the Father has made with us, His adopting love, and His pledge to provide us with all the provision and protection of a loving father. Being baptized into the name of the Son signifies and seals the washing away of sins in the blood of the Son and of being united to His glorious person in His death and resurrection. Being baptized into the name of the Holy Spirit signifies and seals the indwelling of the Holy Spirit and His applying to us all the benefits of the redemption purchased by Christ. In short, baptism reminds us that "all things are yours; whether Paul, or Apollos, or Cephas, or the world, or life, or death, or things present, or things to come; all are yours; and ye are Christ's; and Christ is God's" (1 Cor. 3:21–23).

BY RESPONDING IN FAITH TO WHAT GOD HAS DONE FOR ME IN CHRIST

Of course, there must be more than recognition of what God has done in Christ; there must also be an appropriate response. The only appropriate response is the faith that receives the bounties freely given. In Psalm 116, the psalmist asks, "What shall I render unto the LORD for all His benefits toward me?" (v. 12).

What will I give back in return? How will I repay this great gift? The fact is that you don't pay back; you can't pay back. The wonderful answer to the question "What will I *give*?" is "I will *take*"! "I will take the cup of salvation, and call upon the name of the LORD. I will pay my vows unto the LORD now in the presence of all his people" (vv. 13–14). I benefit from baptism when I learn (and relearn) that in grace, the way to render thanks *to* the LORD is to continue to thankfully receive blessings *from* the LORD.

There is no greater blessing received than the triune name of the Lord into which the person has been baptized. This entails identification with the triune God. God the Father, God the Son, and God the Holy Spirit have a claim on you. In this regard, the apostle is emphatic: "Ye are not your own[!] For ye are bought with a price: therefore glorify God in your body, and in your spirit, which are God's" (1 Cor. 6:19–20). The beneficiary implications of this identification are far-reaching. First, it means that I fully renounce all spiritual enemies and sinful ways:

> I forget my father's house and people who are mine (Ps. 45:10). I have nothing to do any more with idols (Hosea 14:8). I purpose to obey God's commandments and part ways with all evil doers (Ps. 119:115). I deny ungodliness and worldly lusts (Titus 2:12).

Second, I am fully and unreservedly devoted to Jesus Christ as my Lord and Savior (Rom. 6:4). I believe in Him (John 9:38), confess Him (Matt. 10:32), love Him (Ps. 116:1), love His people (1 John 3:14), love His law (1 John 5:3), love His day (Isa. 58:13–14), and love His worship (Ps. 84:10). I love everything about Him and belonging to Him (Song 5:16), and I love to hear of others who love Him (Col. 1:4). I have no greater love or joy than to hear that my children are walking in the truth (3 John 4).

BY RAISING UP COVENANT CHILDREN IN THE FEAR OF GOD

What about my children? The inheritance I have received is large and fair, but what about my family? Does God have anything to say to them? What does God say about them? What place and privilege do they have in the house? The consistent message of Scripture is that God is a God of families. In respect to privilege and blessing, children are dealt with under the representation of their godly father or mother. We often read of a child being blessed because of the faith of a parent (Mark 7:29; 9:23–27; John 4:49–50). When Zacchaeus received and confessed Christ as Savior we read that salvation came to "this house" (Luke 19:9; cf. Acts 11:14; 16:31). This does not mean that those in the house are born again because of the faith of the parent. But it does tell us that in terms of covenant status, privilege, and blessing, God deals with the whole house as represented by the believing parent(s).

Consequently, this means that God *does* have something to say about our children. We are not left to fearful doubt or conjecture concerning the will of God for them. Pierre C. Marcel writes, "[God] sets parents free from the fearful unrest which would haunt them if they were obliged to ask themselves: 'Does God wish to be the Father of my child?' without any reply being afforded them."[3] In baptism, God is making abundantly clear to parent and child that He considers this particular child a member of His covenant, that every provision necessary for the eternal salvation of the child has been made and is fully and freely available to him or her. God has not left Christian parents or their children in the dark. He has made known that His will is for their salvation. If a covenant child is lost at last, then it is not because God was silent or unclear as to His will and it is not because there was nothing in the gospel of Christ for him or her. If children are lost, it is because they have persistently and stubbornly refused the overtures of God's grace. Covenant children have no right to be unbelievers. God has claimed them as His own. To willfully and persistently ignore and reject this claim of God is to break covenant and incur the severest of covenant cursing (Heb. 10:29).

All this means that the triune God has a claim not only on me personally but also on my children.

---

3. Pierre C. Marcel, *The Biblical Doctrine of Infant Baptism* (New York: Westminster Publishing House, 2000), 108.

In baptism He is saying, "They are mine." But He is also saying, "I am entrusting them to your care." This means that especially in a child's early life, the benefits of his or her baptism come, to a large extent, through the parent(s). This clearly entails great parental responsibility. This responsibility, if rightly considered and acted upon, is a great benefit to the parent. Many a man has been sobered by the solemn responsibility entrusted to him of his child's soul. It is one thing to neglect and lose your own soul; it is another thing to be responsible for the spiritual blood of your children (see Luke 16:19–31). This solemn baptismal responsibility includes exemplifying for our children the power of true religion. Parents should be able to say to their children, "Be ye followers of me, even as I also am of Christ" (1 Cor. 11:1). This includes a dependence on the Lord and His grace through daily prayers for the early salvation of our children. Ultimately, however, we must remember that Christ alone can show our children how to be perfect. We show them how to repent when we fail.

This responsibility includes instructing children in essential gospel truths from their earliest days. This will be done after church (especially after witnessing a baptism), at family worship, in regular conversations, in the morning, at bedtime, and whenever opportunity arises. In this way parents will teach their child what baptism teaches. Baptism teaches children that they were born in sin and shaped in iniquity (Ps. 51:5), that they are great sinners (Ps. 25:11), that they are not too young to die (2 Sam. 12:18), and that they must be born again (John 3:7). But baptism also teaches the parent and child that the child is never too young to receive salvation. Parents therefore may expectantly plead for God's salvation to come to their infants. As James Bannerman says, "The work of regeneration by the Holy Ghost is a work which it is as easy for Him to accomplish upon the infant of days as upon the man of mature age."[4]

As soon as children are able to understand, parents should urge them to repent and believe the gospel and make every effort to show them their need of the blood of Jesus Christ and how God has provided this for them in their baptism. It was said of Philip Henry, the father of the famous commentator Matthew Henry, that "in dealing with his children about their spiritual state, he took hold of them very much by the handle of their infant baptism, and frequently inculcated upon them that they were born in God's house, and were…dedicated and given up to Him, and therefore were obliged to be his servants."[5] None of this in itself saves a child, but with the blessing of the Lord, it is nevertheless true, as Robert L. Dabney says: "Where the duties

---

4. James Bannerman, *The Church of Christ* (London: Banner of Truth, 1960), 2:111. See John 3:3, 5, 8.

5. Matthew Henry, *The Miscellaneous Writings of the Reverend Matthew Henry: Consisting of the Life of His Father, Sermons, Tracts, and Biographical Sketches of Eminent Christians and Ministers* (London: Samuel Bagster, 1811), 7:30.

represented in the sacrament of baptism are properly followed up, the actual regeneration of children is the ordinary result."[6]

BY THANKFULLY ACKNOWLEDGING GOD'S COVENANT PROVISIONS

Covenant children who are thus reared ought to be impressed early on with the tremendous benefit they have by virtue of their birth into a Christian home. Before I learned to pray, I was prayed for. Before covenanting with God, God made an eternal covenant with me. Just as the child born into our stately mansion and wealth has many advantages (clothing, nutrition, health care, education) over a child born into abject poverty, so the child born into a covenant home has many spiritual benefits over those who are not (Rom. 3:1–2). This child experiences the pleasant and peaceful atmosphere of the "church in the home." Douglas Bannerman describes the "inner life of the Church" as "an atmosphere of prayer and praise." He says, "From the opening scene of the hundred and twenty in the upper chamber, 'all with one accord continuing steadfastly in prayer,' to the closing scene in this section of the history, where we see 'many gathered together' in the house of Mary 'praying,' the voice of united prayer rises continually

---

6. Robert L. Dabney, *Syllabus and Notes of the Course of Systematic and Polemic Theology* (Richmond, Va.: Presbyterian Committee of Publication, 1927), 799.

in the apostolic Church."[7] So it is in the Christian home—along with instruction, example, discipline, and the very presence of the triune God, there is an atmosphere of prayer and praise.

Chrysostom, the early church father, wrote, "Who are the two and the three met in His name? Is it not the father, and the mother, and the child?"[8] Chrysostom's exegesis of Matthew 18:20 may be suspect, but the thought behind it is perfectly correct. God is a God of our families; "a whole beneficent and redemptive spiritual reality surrounds him, of which the craftsmen are respectively God, his parents, eventually his brothers and sisters, his friends, and the Church."[9]

These early impressions ought to instill in the covenant child a profound sense of thankfulness to the triune God. "How good it was that I was born into the church with all its privileges, with all the means of grace, with the communion of the saints, with those who prayed for me, with those who made their greatest parental concern my spiritual good. It was good to have the protection of Christian restraints in the home. It was good that from a child I have known the Holy Scriptures which are

---

7. Douglas Bannerman, *The Scriptural Doctrine of the Church* (Stoke-on-Trent, England: Tentmaker Publications, 2006), 354.

8. As quoted in Douglas Bannerman, *Scriptural Doctrine of the Church*, 60.

9. Marcel, *Biblical Doctrine of Infant Baptism*, 224.

able to make me wise unto salvation" (See Westminster Larger Catechism, Q. 63). One way to benefit from these baptismal benefits is to acknowledge the Lord's great goodness in giving them and to sincerely thank Him for them (Ps. 116:12; 2 Tim. 1:5).

BY SEEKING A PERSONAL AND SAVING RELATIONSHIP WITH CHRIST

To this point, these outward benefits of baptism are very great. God forbid that we would ever minimize them. They belong to the gifts purchased by the ascended Christ for His people (Ps. 68:18–19; Eph. 4:7–16). But in themselves, these outward benefits do not save. My late minister in Scotland used to say, "Satan does not care how far you go in religion so long as you stop short of a saving transaction with Jesus Christ." It is sobering to think that there will be many baptized people in hell—people who in terms of outward gospel privilege excelled many. And yet for all their outward privilege, they will spend the endless ages of eternity with the devil and his angels and with thieves and robbers and harlots (1 Cor. 6:9–10; Rev. 19:20; 20:15).

Why? Because baptism, precious and beneficial as it is, is not an unconditional guarantee that all who receive its sign and seal savingly possess the grace that is signified and sealed. Just as the beneficial preaching of the gospel is to be received in faith, so it is with baptism. Charles Hodge wrote, "When a man receives the Gospel with a true faith, he receives the blessings which the Gospel promises; when he receives baptism in the exercise of faith, he receives the benefits of which baptism is the sign and seal."[10] The validity of baptism does not rest on personal and actual faith, but on God and His covenant promise. To truly benefit from baptism, however, it must be "improved" by faith.

This brings us to the greatest benefit we must gain from baptism—namely, to seek and find the Lord Jesus Christ by faith. As a young child, and all my life long, I should often and seriously use my baptism to reflect on my present standing with God. Though my forehead has the name of the triune God on it, does my heart remain wedded to the world and the pleasures of sin? Or, have I passed from death to life? Has the blood of Christ—that which was signified and sealed in my baptism—been applied to me by the Holy Spirit? Can I call God Father by regeneration? Is there a new principle of life in me that can only be explained as being made "willing in the day of [His] power" (Ps. 110:3)?

The benefit of such self-examination comes when we become convicted of our spiritually lost state and seek the provisions of the gospel held out to us by baptism. It is here we plead that the Lord would make what we profess to be by baptism a reality for us by regeneration and adoption: "Turn away mine

---

10. Charles Hodge, *Systematic Theology* (Peabody, Mass.: Hendrickson, 2016), 3:589.

eyes from beholding vanity; and quicken thou me in thy way" (Ps. 119:37). "[Lord,] I am thine, save me" (Ps. 119:94). "Turn thou me, and I shall be turned; for thou art the LORD my God" (Jer. 31:18).

At this point, the great benefit of baptism is that in it, God is telling seeking souls that He is willing to hear and answer them in particular. Baptism impresses the truth on seeking souls in a personal and visible way, that *to them*, the Lord is "good, and ready to forgive; and plenteous in mercy unto all them that call upon [Him]" (Ps. 86:5). Baptism itself does not save the sinner, but, as James Bannerman says, "it brings him to the very door, and bids him there knock and it shall be opened unto him."[11] In baptism God promises the sinner, "I solemnly commit to help you every time you ask Me for help."[12] "I will hear you, I will not forsake you, I will be merciful to your iniquities, I will pardon your sin, I will give you a new heart that fears My name. I will remember My covenant. I will be your God, and you will glorify Me."

BY LIVING A DEPENDENT AND THANKFUL LIFE THAT GLORIFIES THE GOD WHO SAVED ME

A life of benefiting from my baptism is a life of dependence on God's gospel provisions in Christ and the application of them to us by the Holy Spirit. The Christian life is not easy. We must contend with

---

11. James Bannerman, *Church of Christ*, 113.

12. Paraphrased from Marcel, *Biblical Doctrine of Infant Baptism*, 110.

the world, the flesh, and the devil as long as we live. Therefore, as long as there are the remains of sin, there will be benefit in the promises of baptism for the sinner saved by grace. Berkhof wrote,

> There are promises for the present and for the future, promises for days of prosperity and for seasons of adversity, promises for the living and for the dying. There are promises of renewed strength for those whose strength seems to fail, promises of courage for the faint-hearted and of rest for the weary. There are promises of guidance through life and of deliverance out of temptations, promises of the support of the everlasting arms and of good cheer for the afflicted and the discouraged, promises of security for storm-tossed souls, promises, too, of an everlasting home for weary pilgrims.[13]

Baptism reminds us of these promises and of God's pledge to perform them whenever we ask Him in faith. It encourages us to pray the promises back to God and to expect His gracious answer. Brakel describes this in the following way: "Lord, behold, here are Thy promises, and here is the seal of the promise, that Thou wouldest fulfil them in me. I now prayerfully expect this, namely, that I, being cleansed, may walk in all purity and holiness. I believe Thy

---

13. Berkhof and Van Til, *Foundations of Christian Education*, 72, 73.

truth, I expect the fulfilment of the promises, and rely upon it."[14]

Further, my life of dependence that glorifies God will include frequent use of the sacraments. My baptism can help me in preparing for the Lord's Supper. Jesus said to Peter, "If I wash thee not, thou hast no part with me" (John 13:8). I can use my baptism to examine whether I have the necessary washing required for a right partaking of the Lord's Supper. Thomas Manton said, "Before the church, none but baptized persons have a right to the Lord's Table.... Before God, none but those who have the fruit of baptism have right to the benefits thereof."[15]

Also, I can benefit from my baptism when I observe the administration of baptism to others. Brakel gives several ways in which this can be done: (1) by observing the wonderful goodness of God in again establishing His covenant with a poor sinner; (2) by considering the magnitude of what is being done ("When a child is baptized, he is exalted by God to a much higher level than an earthly king, so that more than a king is inaugurated"); (3) by reflecting on the solemn manner in which I was once brought before the Lord and surrendered to Him; (4) by convicting you and stirring you up to fulfill your covenant engagements to your own baptized

---

14. Brakel, *Christian's Reasonable Service*, 2:523.

15. Thomas Manton, *The Complete Works of Thomas Manton* (Birmingham, Ala.: Solid Ground, 2008), 5:469.

children; (5) by praying that the Lord would make these children partakers of what is sealed to them; (6) by having your heart go out in love to these children who are now covenant members of the Lord Jesus Christ.[16] And one more from Hodge: "Every time the ordinance of baptism is administered in our presence, we hear anew the voice from heaven proclaiming, 'The blood of Jesus Christ his Son cleanseth us from all sin.'"[17]

In all these ways and probably many others, baptism helps the Christian on his way to heaven. The greatest benefit ever received is Christ Himself. To get Christ is the most precious, valuable, beneficent gift any sinner ever received. This is the design of baptism. Someone might ask, however, "What can baptism give me that I don't already have in the Word?" In short, there is no benefit in baptism that is not in the Word. The seal of baptism is attached to the document of the Word. Yet, we can give the last word here to the Scottish divine, Robert Bruce. What Bruce says concerning the sacrament of the Lord's Supper is equally true concerning the benefit of baptism:

> What then, you ask, is the new thing we get? We get Christ better than we did before. We get the thing which we had more fully, that is, with a surer apprehension than we had before. We get a better grip of Christ now, for by the

---

16. Brakel, *Christian's Reasonable Service*, 2:523.

17. Hodge, *Systematic Theology*, 3:589.

Sacrament my faith is nourished, the bounds of my soul are enlarged, and so where I had but a little grip of Christ before, as it were, between my finger and my thumb, now I get Him in the whole hand, and indeed the more my faith grows, the better grip I get of Christ Jesus.[18]

BY PROCLAIMING THE GOSPEL TO OTHERS

In conclusion, while the title of this book speaks about how *I* can benefit from my baptism, I trust it has been clear that baptism is certainly not a private thing. It occurs in the church; the triune God is covenanting there, the parents and children are covenanting there, and the congregation is covenanting there. It is a momentous occasion. It shows us what God in Christ by His Spirit has done for us and in us. But it also shows us what we are to do for Christ and for others. In many ways, the benefits of baptism are, like circumcision, intended to "spill over" into the lives of those who are still without "hope, and without God in the world" (Eph. 2:12). Abraham and his seed were to be a blessing to the nations (Gen. 22:18; 26:4). "If I had a thousand lives to live," John Brown of Haddington is reported to have said, "and a thousand children, I would willingly give them all to promote the conversion of sinners and

---

18. Robert Bruce, *The Mystery of the Lord's Supper* (Richmond: John Knox Press, 1958), 85.

the advancement of Christ's kingdom in the world, as this appears by far the noblest end of my being."[19]

The nature of the New Testament sacraments speaks of their suitability for a worldwide religion. To eat the Passover, it was necessary to go to Jerusalem. For males to be circumcised, it was necessary to come to the temple with a sacrifice. No such restrictions belong to baptism and the Lord's Supper.[20] No restriction remains, either in gender or in place. The call of the gospel is now entirely unfettered and extends to one and all, far and near, "Repent, and be baptized every one of you in the name of Jesus Christ for the remission of sins" (Acts 2:38). Baptism should thus help us promote the glory of the triune God by leading others to see His glory even as we proclaim His praises.

---

19. As quoted in Thomas Houston, *Works Doctrinal and Practical of Thomas Houston DD* (Edinburgh: Andrew Elliot, 1876), 3:122.

20. Douglas Bannerman, *Scriptural Doctrine of the Church*, 243.